JIMMY CARTER

On the Road to Peace

A People in Focus Book

by
Caroline Lazo

Dillon Press
Parsippany, New Jersey

P e o p l e

For Stevie, Peter, and Chip

To work for better understanding among people, one does not have to be a former president sitting at a fancy conference room table. Peace can be made in the neighborhoods, the living rooms, the playing fields, and the classrooms of our country.

— *Jimmy Carter*

Photo Credits
Front Cover: The Bettmann Archive.
Back Cover: Rob Nelson/Black Star.

Cartoon, p. 70; Reprinted by permission: Tribune Media Services.
Illustration, p. 12: Eva Lucero Wilson. Map, p. 88: Ortelius Design.

AP/Wide World: 19, 29, 37, 57, 110. The Atlanta Constitution/Elizabeth
Kurylo: 116. The Bettmann Archive: 51, 53, 59, 61, 64, 76, 79, 84, 93, 111,
119. Courtesy, Jimmy Carter Library: 15, 97, 107. Photo
Reporters/Colburn: 123. Charles Rafshoon: 23, 25, 27, 39. Sipa
Press/Shone: 113. Sygma/Arthur Grace: 82; Richard Melloul: 100. © 1971
Time, Inc.: 46.

Library of Congress Cataloging-in-Publication Data
Lazo, Caroline Evensen.
    Jimmy Carter: on the road to peace/by Caroline Lazo.
    p.   cm.—(A people in focus book)
    Includes bibliographical references and index.
    Summary: A biography of the thirty-ninth president of
the United States who has also served as a human rights
leader, peace negotiator, and presidential advisor.
    ISBN 0-382-39262-0 (LSB).—ISBN 0-382-39263-9 (pbk.)
    1. Carter, Jimmy, 1924– —Juvenile literature. 2. Presidents—
United States—Biography—Juvenile literature. [1. Carter, Jimmy, 1924–
. 2. Presidents.] I. Title. II. Series.
    E873.L39 1996
    973.926'092—dc20
    [B]   95–25513

Cover and book design by Lisa Ann Arcuri

Published by Dillon Press
A Division of Simon & Schuster
299 Jefferson Road, Parsippany NJ 07054
First Edition
Printed in Mexico
10 9 8 7 6 5 4 3 2 1

Contents

	Introduction	8
1	"Away Down South in Dixie"	13
2	School Days	21
3	The Navy Challenge	28
4	A Change in Course	33
5	"Dixie Whistles a Different Tune"	42
6	A Candidate with a Dream	47
7	"Nobody's Perfect"	55
8	At Home in the White House	62
9	Wins and Losses	72
10	Victory at Camp David	86
11	Counting the Days	95
12	Facing the Future	103
13	World Peace Carter Style	109
14	Habitat for Humanity	118
	Selected Bibliography	125
	Index	127

INTRODUCTION

At the end of their terms in office, most American presidents have looked forward to a life of ease—recently symbolized by a golf course, a lake shore, or a quiet bridle path beneath a California sun. But not so for James Earl Carter, the thirty-ninth president of the United States, known around the world as Jimmy.

With the possible exception of John Quincy Adams, who served 17 years in Congress after leaving the White House, Jimmy Carter is the most effective former president in American history. From Nicaragua to North Korea, he has helped to settle disputes, monitor elections, report human rights crimes, and bring about peace wherever he can. His critics claim that he's trying to right the wrongs of his presidency and improve his image for posterity. But others, including renowned statesman Henry Kissinger, denounce such views and often praise Carter publicly. "He wants nothing for himself," Kissinger said in a 1995 television interview. "He is simply dedicated to serving his country . . . a true missionary of peace."

Much was achieved during Carter's presidency—from energy conservation and renewed relations with

China to historic talks at Camp David with the leaders of Israel and Egypt, ancient rivals in the Middle East. But when 52 innocent Americans were seized and held hostage in Iran, a cloud fell over Carter's administration and never went away. His rescue operation failed, and his efforts at quiet negotiation to free the hostages dragged on through his last day in office. Then after months of nonstop diplomacy, Carter's efforts paid off: In January 1981, as Ronald Reagan was sworn into office, the hostages were set free. So it was President Reagan, not Carter, who shared the hostages' spotlight when they returned home.

Was the timing of the hostages' release a pre-arranged political coup by Reagan? If the hostages had been freed a few months earlier—while Carter was still president—would he have been reelected? People polled at the time said "yes." But Carter himself is too busy to ponder such questions, too busy to look back. Firmly grounded in the present, he is doing his best to help build a peaceful world for future generations.

When he is not meeting with leaders around the globe, Carter can be seen on construction sites where he and many other volunteers of Habitat for Humanity are building houses for people in need. Or he might be found in meetings with the scholars and experts who staff the Carter Center in Atlanta, Georgia, where problems such as human rights violations and urban poverty are studied. Or he could be at home in Plains, Georgia, the small town south of Atlanta, where he grew up—and where he met and married Rosalynn Smith, his devoted wife and partner.

Family love and Christian faith have been Carter's sources of strength since childhood. His parents, who held opposing views on racial segregation, instilled in their son a deep respect for people's differences and a firm belief that almost all human conflicts can be solved peacefully.

Carter's positive attitude and personal charm have opened doors that had been closed for centuries, and his famous smile has become a symbol of optimism and sincerity everywhere. As one young boy in Detroit said after President Clinton failed in 1994 to negotiate an end to the professional baseball strike, "Why didn't he send in Jimmy Carter?"

i *n* *F* *o* *c* *u* *s*

Jimmy Carter

Chapter
1

"A way Down South in Dixie"

*I*n 1864, 60 years before Jimmy Carter was born in Plains, Georgia, the blood of Civil War soldiers covered the landscape of America's Deep South—better known in those days as Dixie.

Hundreds of thousands of Confederate soldiers fought to preserve slavery, a way of life that dated back to the sixteenth century, when the first slaves were brought to the South from Africa. By the 1860s Southern landowners were willing to see their farms become killing fields rather than face a change in the status quo. And their determination could be heard in "Dixie's Land," Daniel Emmett's popular song that became the battle cry of the South.

> *In Dixie land, I'll take my stand,*
> *To live and die in Dixie,*

"Away Down South in Dixie"

Away, away,
Away down South in Dixie.

The Civil War finally ended in 1865; the North won, and slavery was abolished in the United States. But in Georgia and throughout the Southern states, attitudes toward black Americans were slow to change. Though buying and selling slaves was made illegal, most landowners and other white citizens still considered black people to be second-class at best, and they continued for decades to segregate them. (Not until the late 1950s, when Dr. Martin Luther King, Jr., aroused the conscience of the country, would attitudes begin to change.)

In the 1920s even most broad-minded white families found it difficult, if not impossible, to alter their deeply rooted feelings about black people. When blacks entered the homes of whites, for example, they still had to use the back door—as they had done all their lives. Like an addiction, segregation had taken hold in the South and seemed impossible to conquer.

At that time, southerners who ignored the race barrier—and judged people by their character, not their color—were rare exceptions to the rule. But without even trying, in their day-to-day behavior toward neighbors, employees, and strangers alike, such people

Jimmy Carter

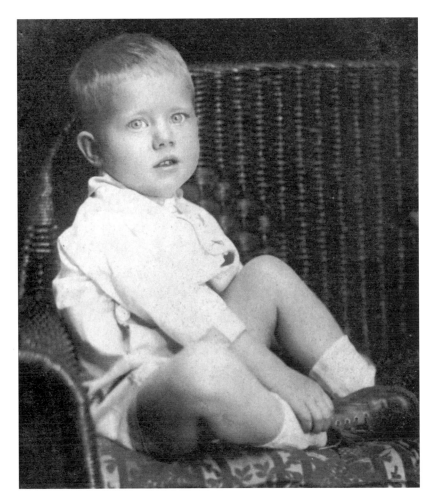

James Earl Carter, Jr., as a young child

helped to change the psyche of the South. In the little rural town of Plains, Georgia, Lillian Gordy Carter, who was affectionately called Miss Lillian, was one of those southerners who were not influenced by considerations of race. Her very existence was an example of a world without prejudice, a world without fear. And her influence on her first-born son, Jimmy, would be profound.

Jimmy Carter, christened James Earl Carter, Jr., was born in Plains on October 1, 1924. His father, James Earl Carter, Sr., was known around town as Mr. Earl. He was a fourth-generation Carter in Georgia, but he was the first to make the family name a household word in Plains.

Earl found many ways to make money in town, but the enterprise that lasted the longest was the farm in Archery, a small community a few miles away. Though primarily a peanut farm, other crops—cotton, corn, and sugar cane—were grown there, too. The farm was a family business, and by the age of 13, Jimmy had learned how to clean, roast, and store peanuts. He had also learned to make a big profit when he sold them in town, even at the low price of five cents a bag! No wonder his father called him "hot shot." In *Everything to Gain,* written years later by Jimmy and his wife

Rosalynn, he explains the importance of tackling challenges and taking risks at a young age.

> *Since I was a young boy, the thrust of my prayers— at least when I was trying to make a good impression on God—has always been that I not fail to use fully and effectively the one life I have on earth. I have always enjoyed difficult challenges. At the same time I have [realized] that it is not easy to take a chance or confront the prospect of failure or embarrassment. But my feeling is that if we refuse to try something that might fail, we lack faith either in ourselves or in our . . . goals.*

Jimmy's younger sisters and brother—Gloria, Ruth, and Billy—shared both the fun and hardships on the farm. Even though the Carters were more fortunate than most residents of the rural South, they had no electricity, running water, heat, or telephone when Jimmy was very young. But when they finally received electricity (in 1937), the Carters bought a radio, and friends and neighbors throughout the community would come over to hear news from the outside world. Their large clapboard house was usually filled with friends and activity . . . and lasting values, too, as Carter later described in *Everything to Gain*.

"Away Down South in Dixie"

On a farm or in a small rural community . . . it was impossible to live a life of isolation from our neighbors. We share almost everything, including a lot of knowledge about specific skills. For example, if something was broken, we usually had to fix it ourselves . . . Much of what we do now comes from that background.

By the time he was a teenager, Jimmy had many friends, including the black children he had grown up with. It was always their friendship that mattered to him, not the color of their skin. They swam together, fished together, and played games together, and remained friends all of their lives. But Earl Carter, with generations of prejudice in his blood, never socialized with blacks. When they came to visit his children or his wife, he automatically left the house. Though he gave his black farm workers food and shelter and treated them kindly, he never mixed with them—or any black people—after work. And they never expected him to. "Certainly by today's standards, my father was a segregationist, as were all the white citizens of the area, so far as I knew," Jimmy Carter recalled in *Turning Point*, published in 1992.

Jimmy's mother, however, not only invited black friends to her home but, as a registered nurse, often treated their injuries and illnesses there. Though she,

Jimmy Carter

Jimmy Carter as a teenager

too, had been raised in the heart of Dixie, her Christian beliefs were deeper than her roots in the South. To her, all human beings were children of God and their color was irrelevant. "When her black friends came to our home," Carter remembered, "she encouraged them to come through the front door, and . . . she treated them as equals."

His mother's genuine fairness toward blacks made a lasting impression on young Jimmy Carter. Looking back, he called it "a good lesson." And it didn't surprise Miss Lillian years later when Jimmy, as a submarine officer, strongly favored President Harry S. Truman's order to end racial discrimination in the United States armed forces.

But how could parents with such opposite points of view live together happily under the same roof? How could a husband who harbored such deep racial bias stand to see his wife welcome blacks into their house—and through the front door? "This was one of the few issues on which she defied my father—not blatantly, but in her quiet and persistent way," Carter said about his mother in *Turning Point*. And his father, he said, "had to learn not to acknowledge this breach of a rigid custom when it occurred."

Little did his parents realize that their attitudes—and the calm way they dealt with their differences—were shaping the character of a future president of the United States.

Chapter
2

School Days

When Jimmy Carter started school, the world was entering the Great Depression. Banks failed to function, people lost their jobs, and hunger was almost everywhere. The Carters were more fortunate than most because they had their farm and their savings to support them. They also had the moral support of the Plains Baptist Church, where Earl Carter was a deacon and the family members attended faithfully. And as Jimmy soon realized, he was lucky to have a mother who loved to read.

Miss Lillian taught Jimmy to read when he was only four, and by the age of twelve he was reading Leo Tolstoy's *War and Peace*, which is almost a thousand pages long. Even when he discovered it was about Russia during Napoleon's invasion in 1812 and not about America's Wild West as he had thought, he kept on reading the book and learning from it. "War on the one hand is such a terrible, such an atrocious thing," Tolstoy wrote, "that no man . . . has the right to assume the responsibility of beginning it."

Jimmy's favorite teacher in school, Julia Coleman, taught him about art and music and encouraged him to enter spelling contests and school debates. While on the debate team, he joined discussions on a subject familiar to him—war and peace. At the time, in the late 1930s and early 1940s, Europe was suffering under Hitler's domination, and the United States was debating the pros and cons of sending aid to its allies there. On one issue, however, there was no debate as far as Jimmy was concerned: If the United States had to enter the war, Jimmy wanted to join the Navy . . . just as his uncle, Miss Lillian's brother Tom, had done years before.

Although Jimmy played baseball and basketball, he claims he wasn't good at either. It was a different story on the running track, where he ran fast and skillfully. He also excelled academically and was at the top of his class. In fact he was certain to be the class valedictorian on graduation day. But as that day approached in 1941, the 16-year-old Carter was tempted by some

Jimmy Carter

Jimmy Carter is shown here (lower right) *in a high school class picture.*

friends to skip school for a day. They were good students, so they thought their absence wouldn't matter. It did. They were reprimanded, and Jimmy's chance to be valedictorian was lost. But his teacher did give him a chance to read a speech at their graduation because she knew he enjoyed public speaking and was good at it.

Graduation from Plains High School by no means meant the end of studying. In fact the toughest courses were about to begin. To fulfill his dream of entering the United States Naval Academy at Annapolis, Maryland, Jimmy had to take a course in chemistry. So he was admitted to Georgia Southwestern Junior College in Americus, Georgia, where he studied chemistry and engineering and even played basketball on the first team there.

He continued his studies at Georgia Institute of Technology and joined its Navy Reserve Officers Training Corps (ROTC). Again he rose to the top of his class, and in 1943, at age 19, his dream came true: He received a congressional appointment to Annapolis and began his training at the Naval Academy that year. Though he was only 5 feet 9 inches tall and weighed only 155 pounds, he proved that height and weight matter little when it comes to learning electronics, naval sciences, and flying skills—all of which Jimmy Carter mastered at the Academy.

Traditionally, upperclassmen would badger new cadets and make life as tough as possible for them. And young Jimmy Carter was no exception. Of course, it

Midshipman James Earl Carter at Annapolis

never dawned on his superiors that "the new cadet with the big smile" would be *their* superior someday. At the time, Jimmy was just another cadet—and was told to lose the smile and get to work! He worked hard and, like most cadets, looked forward to going home on leave to see his family. One visit in particular would become unforgettable.

While Jimmy was on leave in 1945, his sister Ruth "re-introduced" him to her friend Rosalynn Smith. Though Rosalynn's family had been friends of the Carters for years, Jimmy had been so busy as a young boy working on the farm in Plains, playing with his friends, and doing homework that he hadn't noticed the beautiful girl growing up next door. (Her beauty, he said later, is a reflection of her compassionate spirit.)

Rosalynn, too, came from a hard-working family. Her father, who had been an automobile mechanic, died when she was only 13. Her widowed mother, Allie Murray Smith, worked at the Plains Post Office to support her four children, and Rosalynn worked in a beauty shop before entering college nearby. (It was Miss Lillian who helped care for Mr. Smith and comforted his family when he was dying of leukemia.)

In *Always a Reckoning* Jimmy recalls his early attraction to Rosalynn. "Within a crowd, I'd hope her glance might be for me, but knew that she was shy, and wished to be alone." But maybe Jimmy was a little shy, too, because in an interview with Forrest Sawyer on ABC-TV, in January 1995, Rosalynn confessed: "I tried to get him to date me for a long time!"

Once they started dating, they never stopped, and on July 7, 1946—one month after he graduated from

Rosalynn and Ensign Jimmy Carter after their wedding in July 1946

the Naval Academy—Jimmy and Rosalynn were married in Plains. A whole new journey was about to begin.

Chapter
3

*T*he Navy Challenge

*C*arter's graduation from the United States Naval Academy marked the beginning of his eight years of service in the Navy. Though the couple often spent weeks apart while Jimmy was at sea, Rosalynn kept busy with their growing family: John William (Jack), born July 3, 1947; James Earl III (Chip), born April 12, 1950; and Donnel Jeffrey (Jeff), born August 18, 1952.

World War II had ended in 1945, so Jimmy looked forward to learning more about new naval equipment and programs. His service included duty in Portsmouth, Virginia; New London, Connecticut; and Hawaii. It was in Hawaii that he first served on a submarine, the U.S.S. *Pomfret*. And in New London he was the senior officer in charge of the building of U.S.S. *K-1*, the first United States submarine to be built after World War II. Then in 1952 Carter met the biggest challenge of all—serving under Captain Hyman Rickover, head of the Navy's nuclear submarine division.

Lieutenant Jimmy Carter (second from left) *aboard the U.S.S.* K-1 *in 1952*

Before he began his assignment as senior officer on the second nuclear submarine, the U.S.S. *Seawolf*, Carter was asked a battery of questions by Rickover. He wanted to know what Carter had gained from his training. One question was typical of Rickover: "Did you always do your best?" When Carter confessed he had not always done so, Rickover snapped back: "Why not?" Carter had no answer, and the question haunted him for years. Nonetheless, Rickover accepted Carter in the nuclear submarine program, and Carter later acknowledged the profound effect Rickover had on his life, perhaps second only to that of his father. In 1975 the Carter family was not surprised when Jimmy titled his autobiography *Why Not the Best?*

Carter also admired United States President Harry S. Truman (1945–1953), who ended racial segregation in the armed forces. Since his early childhood in Plains, where most of his friends were black, Carter had been sensitive to the unfair treatment blacks received in the South. But in the Navy he discovered that discrimination was not limited to the southern states or to the United States. In *Turning Point* he recalled an incident in the Caribbean that he would never forget.

While I was serving on the U.S.S. K-1 . . . we went into port in Jamaica for some brief shore leave. . . . I happened to be the officer of the deck when [we] received an invitation from the British governor-general to a party in honor of our ship's visit. The aide who delivered the message told me that many of the young ladies in the community would be joining us for the evening. The officers and men were overjoyed. . . . The same aide soon returned with a confidential message: The governor-general did not, of course, mean for our black crewmen to attend the ball. . . . When I informed our captain, William Andrews, he was dismayed. I suggested that we let the crew decide how to respond. They voted unanimously . . . in high-ly descriptive language, that we tell the Jamaican officials what they could do with their party.

Carter was proud of the stand he had taken with his captain and his crew. When he returned to Plains and told his parents about it, his mother was proud, too. But his father said, "The governor of Jamaica was absolutely right." The year was 1951, and Jimmy realized that racial bias was too deeply instilled in his father to ever go away. The whole white South seemed to have been brainwashed against blacks.

Yet Jimmy also knew that his father, whom he always called Daddy, had some wonderful traits of character. His generosity to others—especially his farm workers—was famous in Plains. Mr. Earl had either started or supported every civic project that benefited the people of Plains. He had served in the church and on the Board of Education. And in the Georgia House of Representatives, he had focused on vocational education as a route to jobs and self-esteem.

Those were things Jimmy admired about his father. And when Earl Carter died of cancer on July 23, 1953, at the age of 59, his son faced a major turning point—one that changed the course of his life.

Chapter
4

A Change in Course

Rosalynn was content as a Navy wife, and she enjoyed seeing the world outside of Plains. But she knew Earl Carter's death would cause her husband to rethink his plans for the future. She urged him to stay in the Navy, but his father's death had left a vacuum at home, and Jimmy knew he was needed there. Someone had to run the family farm and try to fill the leadership role his father had held for so long in the community.

After much discussion, Jimmy prevailed. A reluctant Rosalynn accepted the decision, and Lieutenant Senior Grade Jimmy Carter resigned from the Navy. In the fall of 1953, they packed their bags and with their three boys (Jack, Chip, and Jeff) returned to Plains.

Soon after their arrival, Jimmy enrolled in business and agricultural courses to learn as much as possible about running the farm. His mother and younger brother Billy joined him in the operation of Earl Carter's peanut farm and warehouse, and Rosalynn did the bookkeeping. Not more than 30 families lived in Archery, and life there revolved around the Carter businesses. All the social activities, including school and church functions, took place in Plains two miles away, just as they had when Jimmy was a boy.

By 1963 the Carter enterprises were making a million dollars a year, and Jimmy was as well-known in Plains as his father had been. And like Mr. Earl, he proudly served on the board of the Plains Baptist Church, where he was greeted warmly by everyone.

But one day when Jimmy was out of town, the church officers decided to vote on whether to stop blacks from attending Sunday services. When he heard about it, Jimmy rushed home to vote "no." Yet in the end the majority ruled, and blacks were banned from all services except funerals. Jimmy promptly resigned his post as deacon of the church; he wanted no part of the racism there.

When Jimmy became a member of the local school board, he had to face the issue of race again; this time it related to the freedom of blacks to enter white schools. The South still operated under the old "separate but equal" rule of 1896. At that time the Supreme Court had ruled that railroads could insist on whites and blacks riding in separate train cars as long as they were equal in comfort and equipment. In the 1950s, however, the blacks were still riding in separate railroad cars, going to separate schools, and attending separate churches—and nothing about those facilities was equal to those for the whites! Jimmy always wondered why things should be separate for blacks in the first place.

"In my school board work," he wrote in *Turning Point*, "I had become increasingly frustrated with the policies imposed on us by the state government, and I could envision playing a role in shaping . . . decisions in Atlanta [Georgia's capital] that could help the public school system in Sumter County [including Plains]. It seemed likely also that . . . with Carl Sanders as our next governor, there was the prospect of a more enlightened environment in dealing with racial issues."

So following in his father's footsteps again, Jimmy Carter decided to run for a seat in the Georgia Senate, where he would represent seven counties. But not everyone thought the political arena was right for him.

In *Why Not the Best?* Carter remembers a pivotal conversation with a Baptist minister who was visiting his mother.

> The pastor was surprised that I would consider going into politics, and strongly advised me not to become involved in such a discredited profession. We had a rather heated argument, and he finally asked, "If you want to be of service to other people, why don't you go into the ministry or into some honorable social service work? . . . I retorted, "How would you like to be the pastor of a church with 80,000 members?" He finally admitted that it was possible to stay honest and at the same time minister to the needs of the 80,000 citizens of the 14th senate district.

But when the election was over and the votes were all counted, Jimmy learned just how dishonest some politicians can be. Joe Hurst, a campaign worker for Carter's opponent, Homer Moore, not only had cornered people at the polls and urged them to vote for Moore, but he also had stuffed the ballot boxes with votes from dead people! Because of the fraud, which was discovered after Jimmy lost the election, a new count was taken, and Carter won. So in January 1963, he began his new career in politics as a state senator. His office was in the state capital in Atlanta, where he worked diligently to oppose segregation of blacks, extra benefits for politicians, and waste in government.

Carter plays football with two of his three sons in Plains, Georgia, in 1965.

As he pursued those issues for four years, it became clear that State Senator Jimmy Carter welcomed challenges and was always eager to take on more. As one voter said, "What in the world is Jimmy Carter going to do next?" A few years later Carter would answer that question.

In 1966 he announced his candidacy for governor of Georgia. Though he campaigned hard for the office, his opponent, Lester Maddox, was better known around the state. Often when Jimmy's name was mentioned, people would ask, "Jimmy who?" Also, while serving in the state Senate, Carter had courageously defended desegregation—something Maddox abhorred and vigorously campaigned against. It was an issue many Georgians were afraid to face; racial segregation had been familiar to them for so long. Finally, after a confusing election in which no one candidate won a majority of votes, the state legislature chose Maddox to be the governor.

Saddened by his defeat, Carter turned to his sister Ruth and their Christian faith. From both he gained a new perspective on his loss as well as motivation to carry on. "I waited about a month," he recalled, "and then began campaigning again for governor. . . . I did not intend to lose again."

The four years between 1966 and 1970 were full of activity for Rosalynn and Jimmy Carter. They both traveled around the state to meet the people and listen

Carter campaigning for governor in 1970

to their problems. Jimmy was elected district governor of the International Lions Club—the only source of community functions in many of Georgia's small, rural towns. Later he became chairman of all six regional district governors. He made 1,800 speeches during the four-year period and shook hands with more than 600,000 people! Not even the birth of their daughter, Amy Lynn, (October 19, 1967) could stop the Carter momentum. In fact, Amy added joy to the campaign and spurred the candidate on. With his family so solidly behind him, Carter felt he could overcome any obstacle and win.

During the campaign an Atlanta newspaper editor—who supported Carter's opponent, former Governor Carl Sanders—unfairly called Carter "an ignorant and bigoted redneck peanut farmer." Such untrue publicity hurt him among black voters, who began to wonder about his background and principles. Yet Carter won the election. And when he was sworn in on January 12, 1971, he made his principles and priorities clear to all.

> *Our people are our most precious possession. We cannot afford to waste the talents and abilities given by God to one single person. . . . Every adult illiterate, every school dropout, and every untrained retarded child is an indictment of us all. . . . If Switzerland and Israel . . . can eliminate illiteracy, then so can we. . . . At the end of a long campaign, I believe I know the people of this state as well as anyone. Based on this knowledge of Georgians north and south, rural and urban, liberal and conservative, I say to you . . . the time for racial discrimination is over.*

Even his own campaigners were stunned when Carter called for an end to racial discrimination; it was the first time in the state's history that a governor had done so.

While campaigning, Carter had had to soft-pedal civil rights issues in order to win the election. But now that he was in office, would he really end segregation in Georgia? Could he? Most voters felt it was impossible to do so and that he would ignite incredible opposition if he tried. They had voted for Carter because he was fair-minded, smart, and caring. They would soon discover he was also a man of his word.

One thing was sure: From then on, when Georgians heard the name Jimmy Carter, they would no longer say, "Jimmy who?"

Chapter
5

"Dixie Whistles a Different Tune"

*O*nly 120 miles separated the Carter home in Plains and the governor's mansion in Atlanta. But the lifestyles were light-years apart. "It was a huge house," Chip Carter said, remembering the move to Atlanta. "A great place to bring a date!"

The Carters had to adjust to much more than a large, formal house; they had to get used to a whole new life in the public eye. But on weekends they could escape from city life and visit "the naturally beautiful areas of the state," as the new governor recounted in *Why Not the Best?*:

Our favorite place was Cumberland Island . . . where one can see dozens of sea turtles coming ashore to lay their eggs in the early summer. We would watch the sun rise over the Atlantic, and drive down twenty miles of the broad white beach without seeing another living soul.

Long before the environment became a global issue, Jimmy Carter made its importance known in Georgia. He worried about the encroaching land development along the "beautiful, wild" Chattahoochee River near Atlanta, where muskrats and wood ducks had lived for centuries. "It would be a bitter shame," he wrote, "if all this natural beauty were not preserved."

Governor Carter also felt strongly about the accurate preservation of Georgia's history—especially as it was displayed in the capitol. Thousands of children visited the building each week, but until Carter became governor, they had seen only portraits of white leaders on its walls. This was wrong, Carter believed, because black people had made history in Georgia, too. "As both a substantive and symbolic gesture," he wrote in *Why Not the Best?*, "I decided to select several notable black citizens and honor them by hanging their portraits in the State Capitol." He began with the portrait of Dr. Martin Luther King, Jr., a Georgian devoted to racial harmony but who had been assassinated in 1968.

At the unveiling ceremony in the Capitol on February 17, 1974, Secretary of State Ben Fortson spoke glowingly of Dr. King's achievements. Members of the racist Ku Klux Klan paraded in protest outside, and Lester Maddox vowed he would win the governorship in 1974 and take King's portrait down. (Carter wrote later that Maddox was soundly trounced in the 1974 election.) The audience at the ceremony inside ignored the few voices of opposition and listened intently to Secretary of State Fortson's tribute to King. Blacks and whites joined in singing "We Shall Overcome," the theme of the civil rights movement, which King had founded.

Carter summed up the ceremony in *Why Not the Best?*

This was a small gesture in a way, the hanging of these portraits [including those of Bishop Henry McNeal Turner and Lucy Laney], but it seemed especially significant to those who had assembled for the ceremony. It seemed that everyone was aware of how far we had come during the last few years [and] of how far we had to go . . . [but] no matter what the future holds we must face it together.

Jimmy Carter brought out the best in both black and white citizens—not through lectures and orders but, like his mother, through his personality and his faith in his fellow human beings. He expected them to try to get along, and they did. Government jobs for blacks increased by 30 percent while Carter was governor. Working together, Carter and his administration eliminated wasteful projects, reorganized government agencies, and reformed Georgia's prison system.

To many citizens, Carter's most innovative solution to a state problem was the creation of the biracial civil disorder unit, which consisted of three state patrol officers. Dressed in plain clothes, the officers would go into neighborhoods where racial clashes were imminent and, through their power of persuasion, bring opposing forces together. Finally, before the unit left a neighborhood, it made sure that a committee of citizens was in place to continue the dialogue and defuse any flare-ups.

The Civil Disorder Unit was an important success; by 1973 only 177 hours of officers' time per year were needed for racial conflicts in Georgia. Before Carter took office, the number of hours logged for such conflicts had reached 45,910! Other states took notice of the unit's success, and soon the CDU became a model for the country. Already Carter was proving his own credo—that peacemaking is not confined to conference room tables; it can happen in the neighborhoods of our country.

Carter never intended to be the "integration governor." He simply acted according to his own sense of fairness and the early lessons he had learned from Miss

Lillian, Julia Coleman, the Bible, and other great books. To him, all human beings were children of God and should be treated equally—according to their character, not their color—as his mother had always done.

Carter's policies that brought blacks and whites together in Georgia caught the attention of the national media. In May 1971, *Time* magazine featured him on its cover with the headline, "Dixie Whistles a Different Tune." Other magazines hailed him as the messenger of a New South. Some even began to wonder, will he run for president?

In 1974, when Carter's term as governor ended, he answered that question. "Yes!"

Georgia Governor Jimmy Carter appreared on the cover of Time *magazine, May 31, 1974.*

Chapter
6

A Candidate with a Dream

No one was more aware of Carter's popularity as governor of Georgia than his mother, Miss Lillian. But it never dawned on her—or any member of the family—that in 1974 he might have his eyes on the White House. In fact, when she heard the rumor that her son was going to run for president, she said, "President of what?"

Why would Carter want to leave the state he loved and the governorship that brought him such praise? "To me," he wrote in *Keeping Faith,* "the political and social transformation of the Southland was a powerful demonstration of how moral principles should and could be applied . . . to the legal structure of our society." What had worked in Georgia, he believed, could work throughout the country. But once again he would face the "Jimmy who?" question because, although he had become famous in the South, he was still unknown in most of the United States. The presidential race would certainly be his toughest political challenge so far.

While he was governor, Carter led the 1972 Democratic Governors' Campaign Committee, whose purpose was to help elect Democratic governors around the country. Also, he chaired the Democratic National Campaign Committee in 1974. Both jobs helped to combat the Republican charge that he lacked experience in national politics. In fact, his being an outsider—not a part of the Washington scene—was a plus for Carter in the mid-1970s.

The Watergate scandal, involving the burglary of the Democratic National Headquarters at the Watergate building in Washington, D.C., in 1972, still clouded the atmosphere in Washington, even after Republican President Richard M. Nixon resigned. Corruption among Nixon's officials and cover-up charges against the president himself had led to a threat of impeachment by Congress. Though Vice President Gerald Ford took over as president, the memory of Richard Nixon was hard to erase.

To most Democrats, Jimmy Carter was a fresh breeze sweeping through American politics. "He was

Mr. Clean," wrote Jack Germond of the *Baltimore Sun*. "Morally upright and religious . . . and a masterful politician. He could remember things you said years after meeting him!" Reporters had difficulty finding fault with him, but Carter knew there were some things—including his own stubborness—that could hinder his campaign.

"I don't know how to compromise on any principle I believe is right," Carter wrote in *Why Not the Best?* Ben Fortson, his friend and Georgia's Secretary of State, said Carter could be "as stubborn as a South Georgia turtle." Also, Carter thought that being born and raised in the Deep South might be a big roadblock in his campaign. Not since Andrew Johnson occupied the White House, more than 100 years earlier, had a southerner been elected president. "Yet, I remember," he wrote, ". . . when the political analysts said that Southerners would never vote for an Irish Catholic from Boston, but when the returns were counted in 1960, John Kennedy got a bigger margin of victory—not in Massachusetts but in Georgia!"

Finances posed another large problem for Carter. Other candidates had already raised millions prior to the adoption of new financing laws. To win the nomination and the election, Carter would have to do what he did best—go out and meet the people, shake their hands, listen to their problems, and capture the hearts of thousands of volunteers willing to work tirelessly for his campaign. He had already won over his family and friends, the nucleus of his support.

One good friend, Hamilton Jordan, organized the "peanut brigade"—loyal volunteers from Georgia who traveled at their own expense to help their native son win the presidential race. They began in New Hampshire, where the first crucial primary election was held. They went from house to house to talk about their candidate and what he hoped and dreamed for America. Restoring ethics in government in the wake of Watergate as well as building peace in the world after the Vietnam War (1957–1975) were important issues on the minds of Americans.

Carter's dream for America, as he stated in *Keeping Faith*, was "that his country [would] set a standard within the community of nations of courage, compassion, integrity, and dedication to basic human rights and freedoms." It inspired hope throughout the country. And he repeated it throughout New Hampshire—in factories, schools, churches, stores, government buildings, and even at bus stops. "The most important

mmy Carter
President

Jimmy Carter, holding his daughter, Amy, announces that he will seek the Democratic presidential nomination in 1976.

purpose of all was for me to learn this nation—what it is, and what it ought to be," Carter wrote.

His reading habits hadn't changed since he was a student; he still read several books a week. But now that he was running for president, he was reading more about foreign relations, defense, and economics. He was also studying energy conservation and nuclear disarmament—important topics on America's agenda.

The enviroment was important to Carter, too, as it had been when he was governor of Georgia. But it was the ecology of the whole country that concerned him now, and he didn't hesitate to tell all Americans what he thought. In *Why Not the Best?* he wrote

We are still floundering . . . about protection of our environment. Neither designers of automobiles, mayors of cities, power companies, farmers, nor those of us who simply have to breathe the air, love beauty, and would like to fish or swim in pure water have the slightest idea what is coming out of Washington next! What does come next must be a firm commitment to pure air, clean water, and unspoiled land.

Democratic candidate Carter was ahead of his time again when he attacked the unfair tax system in this country.

When a business executive can charge off a $50 luncheon on a tax return and a truck driver cannot deduct his $1.50 sandwich—when oil companies pay less than five percent on their earnings while employees of the company pay at least three times this rate—when many pay no taxes on incomes of more than $100,000—then we need basic tax reform!

Underlying all of Carter's messages was a plea for compassion and competence in government. In a nation still weathering the Watergate scandal, his call for credibility and trustworthiness in its leaders was welcomed by voters in New Hampshire and in other primary elections around the country.

Carter won 18 primaries, including New Hampshire. And on July 15, 1976, after 400,000 miles of travel and

Presidential nominee Jimmy Carter is surrounded by members of his family at the Democratic National Convention after making his acceptance speech. Left to right are Carter's mother, Lillian; daughter, Amy; son Jack; Carter; wife, Rosalynn; son Jeff; Jeff's wife, Annette; son Chip.

2,000 speeches, he received the Democratic Party's nomination for president of the United States.

Now Carter would compete with Republican nominee Gerald Ford for the highest office in the land. Ford was not only more experienced in national politics but he was already president, since Nixon's resignation. Still, Carter had a dream and was determined to see it come true.

Chapter
7

"Nobody's Perfect"

*C*arter chose Walter Mondale, United States senator from Minnesota, as his vice presidential running mate. In Minnesota, Mondale, too, was called Mr. Clean. Many wondered if two such men could win the election. Their opponents, Republicans Gerald Ford and Robert Dole, had been in Washington for years (Ford, since 1949; Dole, since 1969), yet they remained untainted by the Watergate scandal. Ford claimed that the cleanup after Watergate was under control, and the last thing Washington needed was interference from "an outsider from Georgia." But that didn't stop Carter; it motivated him!

Audiences respected Carter's call for more honesty in Washington and more compassion for those in pain around the world. Young people respected him for believing in—and quoting—the lyrics of his "poet-friend" Bob Dylan.

Hey, hey, Woody Guthrie, I wrote you a song
'Bout a funny ol' world that's a comin' along.
Seems sick an' it's hungry, it's tired and it's torn,
It looks like it's a dyin' an it's hardly been born.

Carter had admired Dylan's poetry and music ever since Chip had introduced it to him years ago in Georgia. At Carter's invitation, Dylan visited the family at the governor's mansion. To Carter, "The Times They Are A-changin'" seemed as appropriate during the presidential campaign as it did during his governorship, and young members of the press enjoyed the "odd couple" aspect of Carter and Dylan. But soon there would be much more for the hungry media to feed on.

In September 1976, less than two months before the presidential election, an interview with Carter appeared in *Playboy* magazine. The article made headlines, because in it Carter confessed he "had felt lust in his heart" during his marriage. Reporters rejoiced; they finally had something juicy to write about Carter. And Republicans were delighted to see the saintly image of Carter begin to blur—until Rosalynn dis-

Jimmy Carter and running mate Walter Mondale wave to the crowd at the Democratic National Convention. With them are their wives, Rosalynn and Joan.

armed them with her response. "I believe he was trying to explain his Christian religion," she told reporters. "God doesn't expect one to be perfect. I think it shows he's human." And she reminded reporters, "Nobody's perfect."

On October 6, 1976, less than a month before the election, the second national debate between Carter and Ford made front-page news. During the debate Ford claimed, incorrectly, that the Soviet Union was not dominating Eastern Europe at that time—nor would it ever do so during a Ford administration. Reporters and voters alike wondered how Ford could be so naive. Many worried about his state of mind. Many more still could not forgive him for having pardoned Richard Nixon, who had lied to the American people and helped to corrupt their government. Those incidents plus his bland personality (and Carter's radiant sense of ethics) were big setbacks for Ford, the experts concluded.

On November 2, 1976, the presidential race ended, and the voting began. Not since 1960, when John F. Kennedy defeated Richard Nixon, had an election been so close. But Carter won. And on January 20, 1977, with Rosalynn at his side, Jimmy Carter stood in front of the United States Capitol in Washington, D.C., and took the oath of office. With his hand on the Bible that Miss Lillian had given him, he was sworn in as the thirty-ninth president of the United States. Family members, friends, and dignitaries there—as well as audiences around the world—listened intently to his inaugural address. The public was eager to know more about the recently unknown farmer from Georgia who had just won the most powerful office in the world. And he told them what he believed.

The American dream endures. We must once again have faith in our country—and in one another. . . . Let our recent mistakes bring a resurgent commitment to the basic principles of our nation, for we know that if we despise our own government we have no future. . . . Our nation can be strong abroad only if it is strong at home, and we know that the best way to enhance freedom in other lands is to demonstrate here that our democratic system is worthy of emulation. . . . We will maintain strength . . . a quiet strength based not merely on the size of an arsenal but on the nobility of ideas. . . . We will fight our wars against poverty, ignorance, and injustice, for those are the enemies against which our forces can be honorably marshaled. . . . We can neither answer all questions nor solve all problems . . . we must simply do our best.

Chief Justice Warren Burger administers the oath of office to Jimmy Carter as Mrs. Carter looks on.

"Nobody's Perfect"

After the inaugural ceremony, the president and Rosalynn Carter, along with their daughter Amy, and sons Jack, Chip, and Jeff and their wives, were ushered into limousines for the traditional 1.2-mile ride from the Capitol to the White House. The ride made history when Carter decided to stop, get out of the car, and flanked by his family, walk the rest of the way!

People lining the streets cheered when they saw their president become "one of them"; the walk became a symbol of the openness and down-to-earth quality of the new Carter presidency. "I felt a simple walk would be a tangible indication of some reduction in the imperial status of the president and his family," he wrote.

The walk was an easy one compared with the many thousands of miles covered during his campaign. Now the questions was, could President Carter keep his campaign promises—to clean up the White House, set high moral standards for his Cabinet and staff, seek human rights and justice for all, and in general make "our democratic system worthy of emulation"?

Jimmy Carter

President Carter and his family walk to the White House following Carter's inauguration.

Chapter
8

*A*t Home in the White House

*C*arter hoped to bring a simpler lifestyle to the White House. He wanted less pomp and more reality. To save energy and money, his staff would no longer ride in chauffeured automobiles; they would drive their own cars to and from work. This change alone prompted cheers throughout the country. Carter himself cut out the fanfare that had followed the president wherever he went. But when people complained of too *little* ceremony, Carter approved the playing of "Hail to the Chief" at certain functions. And he discovered he liked it. "I found it to be impressive and enjoyed it," he said.

Carter tried to keep his children out of the spotlight so that their lives could be as normal as possible.

And they were as close and as helpful to him during his presidency as they had been during the campaign. Chip's contacts with members of Congress in the pre-election days helped Carter become more familiar with procedures there. He sought advice from all family members. "I even derived useful information from Amy," Carter wrote in *Keeping Faith*. "What would improve the lunch program? How could we help children who could not speak English? What was being done to challenge the bright students . . . or to give extra help to the slow ones?"

Both Rosalynn and Miss Lillian were invaluable to Carter. Since the early days in Plains, Rosalynn had been his partner as well as his wife. And she used that experience and expertise in her new role in the White House. "All of us turned to her for sound advice on issues and political strategy," Carter recalled. Rosalynn also continued to work with the mentally ill, as she had done in Georgia.

Miss Lillian, too, was a great asset to her son— especially when called upon to officially represent the president at functions. The public adored her. As a Peace Corps worker in India at the age of 70, she had become a role model for young and old alike. She was always a big hit in groups "where advanced age [was]

Lillian Carter embraces her son after his election as president in 1976.

revered, liberal social views [were] appreciated, and a lively sense of humor [was] tolerated," Carter wrote.

Carter's Cabinet completed his major group of advisors. Vice President Walter (Fritz) Mondale stood out as a trusted friend and astute advisor. "During our four and a half years together," Carter reminisced in *Keeping Faith,* "I never for a moment had reason to

doubt his competence, his loyalty, or his friendship."
Two friends from Georgia—Hamilton Jordan, campaign manager; and Jody Powell, a loyal volunteer
worker—became Carter's chief of staff and press secretary, respectively. Carter was proud of all the
appointments to his Cabinet because they included
blacks, whites, Protestants, Catholics, and Jews, people from all parts of the country and from a variety of
backgrounds. Initially, his very American Cabinet
included the following members:

> Cyrus Vance, Secretary of State
> Michael Blumenthal, Secretary of the Treasury
> Harold Brown, Secretary of Defense
> Griffin Bell, Attorney General
> Cecil Andrus, Secretary of the Interior
> Bob Bergland, Secretary of Agriculture
> Juanita Kreps, Secretary of Commerce
> Ray Marshall, Secretary of Labor
> Joseph Califano, Jr., Secretary of Health,
>   Education and Welfare
> Patricia Roberts Harris, Secretary of Housing
>   and Urban Development
> Brock Adams, Secretary of Transportation

Other close advisors to Carter included Bert Lance,
director of the Office of Management and Budget;

Andrew Young, ambassador to the United Nations; Zbignew Brzezinski, national security advisor; Charles Schultze, chairman, council of economic advisors; and Robert Strauss, special trade representative.

During his years in the White House, Carter's days began early. "Ever since my boyhood days on the farm," he remembered, "I have enjoyed the solitude and beauty of the early morning hours." But not all moments of solitude in the White House would evoke happy memories for Carter: "Although I was surrounded by people eager to help me," he wrote in *Keeping Faith* "my vivid impression of the Presidency remains the loneliness in which the most difficult decisions had to be made."

Carter's first big decision in office—to officially pardon all those who had refused to fight in the Vietnam War—was a positive one. Many had fled the country, and Carter believed it was time for peace and rebuilding—not just in Vietnam but at home, too. Those who had dodged the draft were convinced that the war in Vietnam was a civil war, between the north and south of that country, and that American interference there was morally and legally wrong. (As it turned out, in 1995 some people who were involved in forming American foreign policy during that war admitted, in retrospect, that the dissenters were right.)

Top priorities on Carter's awesome agenda included energy conservation, education, and the elimination of costly, wasteful projects. He was the first American president to establish a Department of Energy. Because of America's dependence on foreign oil supplies, this country was at the mercy of authoritarian governments abroad, and Carter believed it was time to develop our own oil and alternative energy sources. He asked all Americans to focus on energy conservation in their daily lives.

Bypassing Congress, Carter went directly to the people with his call to arms over the increasing prices for foreign oil. For example, he asked families to lower their thermostats and to drive energy-efficient cars. Congress resented his going directly to the people with his message, because it implied that he didn't trust Congress to take quick action. He was right; it took a year and a half for Congress to pass his energy bill—and even then it was a watered-down version of the original one. Still, Carter had united the people in the energy effort, which he called "the moral equivalent of war," a phrase suggested to him by his longtime friend and mentor, Admiral Hyman Rickover. Carter was proud of the achievement in spite of the time it took to get results. In *Keeping Faith*, he described his commitment.

> Despite my frustration, there was never a moment when I did not consider the creation of a national energy policy equal in importance to any other goal we had. . . . When I took office . . . our dependence on uncertain foreign oil supplies had grown to almost 50 percent—about 9 million barrels a day. We were the only developed nation without an energy policy. . . .

An overriding goal of the Carter administration was to put the interests of the people first. There was much to do. When he took office, 8 million people were unemployed in the United States. By mid-1977, unemployment programs—including job and training programs for young people, the continuation of the Comprehensive Employment and Training Act (CETA), and an emergency public works plan—were putting many people back to work. When Carter left office, he felt good about the progress he had made: Nearly 10 million new jobs had been developed, 1 million summer jobs for youth had been created, and 700,000 adults had been placed in job training and public service. Ever since he had worked on the family farm in Georgia, Carter felt passionately about the importance of having a job: "There are few things more debilitating to a person than to be deprived of a job—a chance for self respect, the realization that one's life is meaningful, the ability to nurture and care for loved ones," he wrote. "The creation of jobs was a top priority for me."

Education was another top priority for Carter. He remembered clearly how some of Georgia's most prominent citizens fought hard to keep blacks from attending white schools, and he was determined to see that integrated schools worked successfully. While he was president, he doubled the budget for education, gave more control to local officials, updated the Elementary and Secondary School Act, increased financial aid by 25 percent, and tripled loan plans for college students.

Because of his preoccupation with details and his incredible ability to remember them, Carter gained a reputation for being a "detail freak." Even on television's *Saturday Night Live*, Dan Ackroyd satirized Carter in a sketch about a postal worker who was having trouble with her mail sorter, a "Marvex 3000." She called the White House for help. Carter, played by Ackroyd, answered the phone and calmly told the worker, step by step, how to repair the machine. The audience couldn't stop laughing.

This cartoon of the Carter White House appeared in the Dayton Daily News *in 1976.*

Carter was used to the joking, though in public he rarely—if ever—showed a playful or very humorous side himself. "The peanut farmer who wants to be president" had been a favorite line in the press prior to the election. Cartoonists loved that image and exploited it throughout the campaign. "They had a field day," Carter recalled, "characterizing us as barefoot country hicks with straw sticking out of our ears, clad in overalls, and unfamiliar with the proper use of indoor plumbing."

Once in office, Carter enjoyed erasing the country bumpkin image. Others did, too: ". . . Jimmy Carter was probably the smartest president since Jefferson or Wilson [and] probably was the most diligent," said Robert M. Gates, former director of the Central Intelligence Agency (CIA) in the Bush administration. But his reputation as an outsider in Washington stayed with him. Biographer Douglas Brinkley noted that Carter "gave the impression he didn't want to deal with Congress. He said he was the leader of the American people, not the Democratic party."

Unfortunately, he had to learn the hard way that being an outsider in Washington could do him more harm than good.

Chapter
9

Wins and Losses

*I*n the early 1900s, the United States had built the Panama Canal through a narrow strip of land gained by a treaty with the Central American country of Panama. During the 1960s and 1970s, the two countries argued about a suitable way to govern the Canal, which the United States had controlled since 1903.

At first, relations between the United States and Panama were friendly, but by the time Carter took office, Panama's growing desire for sovereignty was clouding the alliance. Carter believed it was time to deal with the Canal issue in spite of polls that showed 78 percent of the American people—and most of Congress—wanted to keep the Canal under United States control. Carter believed that a fair treaty between Panama and the United States would allow both countries to share control of the Canal until the year 2000, at which time Panama would gain complete control of the waterway. He also believed that the American people had not been told the possible consequences of avoiding the Canal issue. Without a treaty, he reminded citizens and Congress alike, rebellion in Panama was possible. And in the words of Andrew Young, former American Ambassador to the United Nations, "All-out war in Latin America was likely." Yet the obstacles to making a treaty were overwhelming.

To negotiate a treaty, Carter would have to win over both Panamanian dictator Omar Torrijos *and* the Congress of the United States! As one former campaign worker said, "Since he was a boy selling peanuts in Plains, he loved challenges . . . and this one was a doozy." To many of his supporters, this issue marked the beginning of his visible role as a brilliant peacemaker. To Carter, making peace was often more difficult than making war—but obviously more rewarding. And when the principles of equality and fair play were involved, he felt democratic leaders had no choice but to act on those principles. "I decided that we simply could not afford to fail," Carter said. And the Carter "peace machine" began to roll.

After countless meetings between United States and Panamanian officials, Torrijos finally agreed to sign two separate treaties—one dealing with Panama's control of the Canal in 2000; the other dealing with the right of the United States to defend the Canal.

Yet Carter knew that the ordeal was not over. Winning votes in Congress to ratify the treaties would be even harder. As usual, however, Carter forged ahead, as he described in *Keeping Faith*.

> I *spent a lot of my time planning carefully how to get Senate votes. The task force set up for this purpose developed a somewhat limited objective: not to build up an absolute majority of support among all citizens, but to convince an acceptable number of key political leaders in each important state to give their senators some "running room." We worked closely with the individual senators on lists of state leaders, and we brought hundreds of editors, college presidents, political party leaders, elected officials, campaign contributors, and other influential people into the White House for personal briefings by me. I would invite State Department or Pentagon officials to join me, including the highly effective members of the Joint Chiefs of Staff. At times, military uniforms were of great help. . . . Labor unions, business leaders, the Jaycees, garden clubs, religious groups, senior citizens, schoolteachers, Common Cause, and other organizations joined our effort.*

Senators made trips to Panama to learn more facts and to talk to General Torrijos. The General reiterated his desire to maintain friendly relations with the United States and promised to work toward a democratic government for his country. As Congress became better informed, so did its constituents, and more votes for Carter's plan for the future of the Panama Canal seemed probable. But the process was slow, tedious, and tense. While Carter pressed for more votes in Congress, he had to keep Torrijos at bay in Panama. He ran interference on both fronts constantly—right to the end, when the final vote on the second historic treaty was taken. "It was a cliff-hanger for 24 hours," Carter wrote in his diary on April 18, 1978. But he got the votes he needed, and both treaties were ratified. "Now," Carter wrote, "instead of enemies at war over a damaged—perhaps closed—Canal, we and Panama were to be allies, committed to a partnership of operating the crucial waterway for our common benefit." President Carlos Andres Pérez of Venezuela praised the treaties, too, calling them "the most significant advance in political affairs in the Western Hemisphere in this century."

But the sacrifices made in the process were not small. Out of 20 senators who had voted for the treaties while facing reelection in the fall of 1978, only

President Carter and General Omar Torrijos of Panama sign the ratified Panama Canal treaties.

seven were returned for another term. Their courage, however, was not forgotten by Carter. On April 19, 1978, he sent a handwritten letter to each senator who had voted to ratify the treaties.

Jimmy Carter

April, 1978

To Senator _____:

As President, I want to express my admiration for your support of the Panama Canal treaties. Rarely is a national leader called upon to act on such an important issue fraught with so much potential political sacrifice.

On behalf of the people of the United States, I thank you for your personal demonstration of statesmanship and political courage.

Sincerely,

Jimmy Carter

Though the Panama issue occupied much of Carter's attention, other problems continued to confront him. And he was at a loss when it came to the embarrassing situation involving Budget Director Bert Lance, his good friend from Georgia. In the summer of 1977, accusations appeared in the press that Lance had been involved in unlawful practices while he was president of a Georgia bank. The news stunned the Carters, and they began to see just how "outside the loop" they were in Washington. In *Keeping Faith*, he commented, "We first realized the adverse consequences of still being outsiders when we had to face the allegations raised against Bert Lance."

But the news about Lance stunned the public even more. After all, Carter's whole campaign was about honesty, decency, and the restoration of ethics in government. The Carters, meanwhile, stood by Lance, convinced he was innocent of all charges.

To many people it seemed as though the press actually enjoyed the possibility of a big scandal in the Carter administration, whose reputation had been spotless. Reporters seized upon every item that smacked of impropriety in Lance's past dealings and fed them to newspapers across the country. And wherever Carter spoke, he was deluged with questions about Lance, leaving less time for important international topics— including formal recognition of the People's Republic of China, and pursuit of the Strategic Arms Limitation Talks (SALT) agreement with the Soviet Union.

The Lance affair became a heavy burden for the president, yet he refused to take the advice of others and fire his friend. But on September 20, 1977, Carter made a notation in his diary: "I played tennis late in the afternoon with Bert, and he indicated to me that he wanted to resign. I didn't argue with him." The next day, after Lance officially resigned, Carter wrote again in his diary: "Probably one of the worst days I've ever spent."

Budget Director Bert Lance holds up a newspaper clip-ping at the beginning of Senate investigations into his banking practices.

The investigations into Lance's banking practices in Georgia dragged on for months—at a high cost in legal fees as well as in pain endured by Lance and his family. And in the end, proof of alleged illegalities was not found! "The ordeal," Carter wrote, "was terrible for us all. I am just grateful that eventually it turned out all right, and that the Lances were strong enough in their faith not to be destroyed."

Though his Mr. Clean image had been tarnished, Carter's political skills were as polished as ever, and his dealings with Vice Premier Deng Xiaoping of the People's Republic of China and President Leonid Brezhnev of the Soviet Union would further prove his expertise in diplomacy.

Richard Nixon's historic visit to mainland China in 1972 had paved the way for future recognition of that government by the United States. His trip symbolized the new reality—that the old leader, Chiang Kai-shek, who ruled the Republic of China, based on the island of Taiwan, no longer represented all of the Chinese people on the mainland. But after Nixon's trip, four years passed without any action toward formal recognition of the People's Republic of China. It was Jimmy Carter who finally revitalized relations with China, starting with exchange programs in the arts along with trade and diplomatic relations.

On December 13, 1978, Carter's liaison chief, Leonard Woodcock, met with Vice Premier Deng Xiaoping and formally opened the new road to normal relations between the two countries. Deng welcomed Carter's proposals, and on December 15 the two leaders sent a joint communiqué to their leaders around the world. "The media had been caught by surprise,"

Carter wrote. "Worldwide reaction was remarkably positive," he continued. "Most countries recognized this development . . . would contribute to peace and would open China further to the outside world."

The normalization of relations with China was made official on January 1, 1979, and later that month Deng Xiaoping and his wife visited the Carters at the White House. After a special performance at the Kennedy Center, Carter, Deng, their wives, and the Carter's daughter, Amy, joined the performers on stage. Carter captured the moment in his diary on January 29, 1979.

> *. . . there was a genuine sense of emotion when he [Deng] put his arms around the American performers, particularly little children who had sung a Chinese song. He kissed many of them, and the newspapers later said that many in the audience wept. Senator Lazalt, who has been a strong opponent of normalization, said after that performance that we had them beat; there was no way to vote against little children singing Chinese songs.*

Carter won favorable support in Congress for the new agreement with China, though a few extremist groups strongly opposed recognition of any Communist government, regardless of the peace that it promised. Others, who worried about the loss of

President and Mrs. Carter welcome Chinese Vice Premier Deng Xiaoping to the White House.

trade with Taiwan, were assured that relations with Taiwan would continue through private organizations. "My foreign policy team and I were very proud of our accomplishments," Carter concluded.

Carter hoped that Congress would react as positively to his negotiations with the Soviet Union, America's long-time adversary. Following months of intense preparation in Washington, he met with Soviet President Leonid Brezhnev in Vienna in June 1979. After four days of talks, which included Carter's frank assessment of human rights in the Soviet Union, the two leaders finally signed the SALT II agreement. The treaty's provisions went beyond those of SALT I, and the leaders hoped their agreement would pave the way for SALT III.

In his memoirs, Carter recalled the ceremonial signing in June: "I shook hands with President Brezhnev, and to my surprise, we found ourselves embracing each other warmly in the Soviet fashion. There is no doubt there were strong feelings of cooperation between us at the moment, and I was determined to pursue our search for peace and better understanding." And he credited his achievement to the superb work by his team—Cyrus Vance, Harold Brown, Zbigniew Brzezinski, General David Jones, and retired General George Seigneious.

Back in Washington, Carter stressed the vital importance of SALT II in a speech to Congress.

> *SALT II is the most detailed, far-reaching comprehensive treaty in the history of arms control. . . . For the first time, it places equal ceilings on the strategic arsenals of both sides, ending a previous numerical imbalance in favor of the Soviet Union. . . . but it's more than a single arms control agreement. It is part of a long, historical process of gradually reducing the danger of nuclear war. . . .*

President Jimmy Carter and Soviet leader Leonid Brezhnev sign the Salt II treaty June 18, 1979.

But Carter's hopes for the treaty were soon crushed. The Soviet Union sent invasion forces into Afghanistan in central Asia after a series of military coups there. It was an aggressive action that shocked the world, especially the United States Congress, which was now in no mood to ratify the SALT II treaty or *any* agreement with the Soviets. Carter had no choice but to ask the Senate to postpone the vote. "Our failure to ratify the SALT II treaty and to secure even more far-reaching agreements was the most profound disappointment of my presidency," Carter wrote in *Keeping Faith*. "We can only hope that an aroused public—in the United States and other countries—could convince the leaders of both superpowers that they must work to remove this nuclear shadow [from] over the earth." (When Ronald Reagan later took office, he shelved the SALT II treaty, and the vote to ratify it was never taken.)

Though Carter was disappointed, he was not defeated. He had accomplished a great task. Peace, he always said, did not mean only an end to war. It meant the prevention of more wars by finding ways to get along with one another. With SALT II he had taken a giant step toward that goal. And relations between the Soviet Union and the United States had improved because of it. Human rights violations in the Soviet Union decreased during Carter's presidency, and the number of Jews who were allowed to leave that country more than tripled while he was in office. (It went down dramatically after he left.)

But it was at the presidential retreat of Camp David in the Catoctin Mountains in Maryland that Jimmy Carter's peacemaking would resonate around the world as he brought two ancient enemies together in the most historic event of his presidency.

Chapter
10

Victory at Camp David

*W*hile serving in the Navy during World War II, Jimmy Carter—like most Americans and others around the world—was unaware of the daily tragedies taking place in Hitler's death camps in Europe. Six million of Europe's ten million Jews were gassed, slaughtered, or starved to death in the Holocaust— Hitler's evil pursuit of an all-Aryan world. After the war, survivors of the death camps became refugees, because they had no homes to return to. Jewish populations in Poland, Czechoslovakia, Holland, Greece, and other countries had been wiped out. Some refugees went to Norway, Sweden, Denmark, the United States, and Russia with the hope of building new lives there.

In 1948, when the United Nations created the State of Israel in the Middle East on the Mediterranean Sea, Jews at last had an official homeland. But their new nation was surrounded by Arab states which, since Biblical times, had claimed the land as their own.

Before Israel became a State, it was part of a larger area called Palestine (or the Holy Land). The Palestinians, whose Arab ancestors had settled in the region hundreds of years earlier, resented the Israelis who moved into their territory and treated the long-time residents like enemies. Violent clashes between the Arabs and the Jews became a part of daily life in the area. Yet, in recent wars with their neighbors, Israeli forces triumphed. They managed to hold on to their homeland and occupy the Gaza Strip, the Sinai Peninsula, the Golan Heights, the West Bank, and the Arab sector of Jerusalem as well.

Tired of the bloodshed and terrible cost in lives and money, Egypt's President Anwar Sadat made a historic trip to Jerusalem in 1977 in the cause of peace. Many previous attempts at peacemaking in the region had failed, and the possibility of Egypt turning to the Soviet Union for help began to worry president Carter and other foreign leaders, as he revealed in his memoirs.

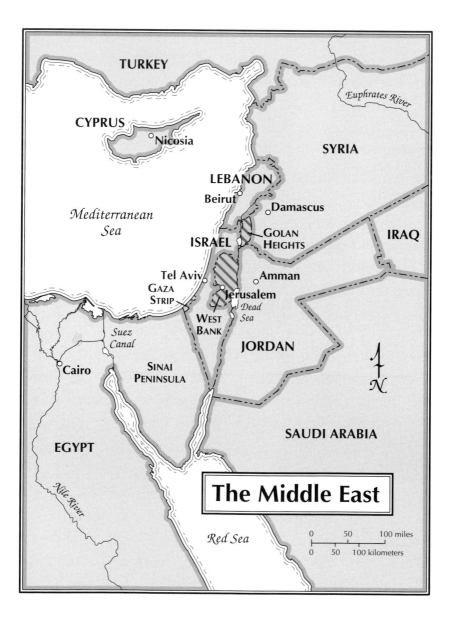

The Middle East

Jimmy Carter

I did not want to drive the Arab leaders away from us and into the arms of the Soviets, so I asked Secretary of State Vance to visit the key countries to assure them that the goal of a comprehensive peace was not being abandoned. . . . Sadat's visit to Jerusalem had broken the Arab shell which had been built to isolate Israeli. . . . However, it was becoming obvious that Sadat and [Israeli Prime Minister] Begin alone could not go very far in resolving the basic problems that had not been touched—the Palestinian issue, the withdrawal of Israeli forces from occupied territory, Israeli security, or the definition of a real peace.

Arab leaders urged President Carter to stay involved in efforts to resolve the Middle East problems. Carter would do that and much more. After months of studying Middle East history and the conflicts there, Carter created a peace plan—not an American plan to be imposed on foreign leaders, but a "framework" in which they could work out a plan of their own. Peace plans, he believed, were successful only when they evolved from "joint negotiations."

Carter discussed his ideas with Vice President Mondale, Cyrus Vance, Zbigniew Brzezinski, Hamilton Jordan, and other close advisors. Because Prime Minister Begin and President Sadat did not get along well alone, Carter and his staff believed that the peace talks could succeed only if the two leaders met in Carter's presence, with Carter in the role of mediator. "I finally decided it would be best, win or lose, to go all out," he wrote in his memoirs. "There was only one thing to do, as dismal and unpleasant as the prospect seemed, I would try to bring Sadat and Begin together for an extensive negotiating session with me."

On August 5, 1978, Carter invited both leaders to meet with him in September at Camp David, the beautiful mountainside retreat in Maryland. The presidential hideaway was the ideal place, Carter felt, for private talks without interruptions.

When Begin and Sadat accepted the invitation, Carter's preparations went into full gear. He studied biographical material that his team of experts had prepared for him about the two leaders. And he researched certain questions regarding the adversaries.

- What had made them national leaders?
- What was the root of their ambition?
- What were their most important goals in life?
- What events had helped to shape their characters?
- What were their religious beliefs?
- What were their family relations?
- What were their relations with other leaders?

■ What were their political beliefs and constraints?

■ What were their strengths and weaknesses?

After studying those questions and more, Carter outlined three parts to an "ultimate agreement" between the president of Egypt and the prime minister of Israel.

First, true peace must be based on normal relations among the parties to the peace.

Second, there must be withdrawal by Israel from territories occupied in 1967 and agreement on secure and recognized borders for all parties in the context of normal and peaceful relations. . . .

Third, there must be resolution of the Palestinian problem in all its aspects. The solution must recognize the rights of the Palestinian people and enable [them] to participate in the determination of their own future.

Carter asked his wife to join him at Camp David because he wanted Rosalynn's "support and advice" throughout the negotiations. And all three leaders would have their own staffs on hand to assist them at the historic event, which began on September 5, 1978.

As expected, Carter found Sadat easy to get along with, but he had some difficulty with Begin's "stubborn streak." At times, Carter would assure the two leaders that their responses to each other were not as negative as they seemed, and he persuaded them to press on.

To relax, the Carters rode their bikes through the woods, accompanied only by birds and surrounded by trees. Such privacy, Carter believed, was essential to ease the tension of the high-powered talks at the Camp.

After 13 days of meetings, which Carter deftly mediated, a "framework for peace" between two ancient enemies, Egypt and Israel, was agreed to. Newspapers around the world called the event "a remarkable victory." And Carter noted in his diary that after the news reached Israel, teachers on strike there were so happy that they stopped the strike and went back to work!

On September 18, the leaders left Camp David and returned to the White House to sign their agreement. It was fitting that on that same afternoon the Carters' good friend Mstislav ("Slava") Rostropovich, renowned cellist, gave a concert at the White House. Rostropovich had recently left the Soviet Union in search of peace and freedom in the United States.

The new framework for peace signed that day was a prelude to the formal peace treaty between Israel and

92

Egyptian President Anwar Sadat, U.S. President Jimmy Carter, and Israeli Prime Minister Menachem Begin clasp hands after the signing of the Mideast Peace Treaty, March 26, 1979.

Egypt, known as the Camp David Accords, which was signed on March 26, 1979, also at the White House. In *Keeping Faith*, Carter reflected on the historic event: "My hope has been that the peace treaty can convince other Arab leaders of the advantages of negotiations in good faith, and that the courage of President Sadat will inspire them and Israeli leaders to make similar bold moves for peace."

Carter knew that the ceremonial signing was just a beginning. For peace to endure in the Middle East, Israel's Arab neighbors would have to accept—in their hearts as well as their minds—Israel's sovereignty. As Carter has said so often, "Peace means much more than an end to fighting."

Later that year President Sadat and Prime Minister Begin jointly won the Nobel Peace Prize for their extraordinary commitment to peace. But to all those involved in Sadat's and Begin's efforts, it was Jimmy Carter who made it all happen.

Chapter
11

Counting the Days

*C*arter's last year in office was haunted by an event out of his control—namely, terrorism in Tehran, the capital of Iran. "Sunday, November 4, 1979, is a date I will never forget," Carter wrote in his memoirs. "Early in the morning I received a call from Brzezinski, who reported that our embassy in Tehran had been overrun by about 3,000 militants, and that 50 or 60 of our American staff had been captured."

When the United States had allowed the deposed shah of Iran to seek medical help in the United States, Iran had retaliated in terroristic fashion. The Iranians hated the shah and wanted him to return to Iran and face questions about the fortune he had made and taken out of the country at the expense of the Iranian people. But the shah's return would mean his certain death in a country run by fanatics out for revenge.

Iran's prime minister made a promise to Carter that the hostages would not be harmed. But he also demanded that the United States return the shah (and his money) to Iran. The fanatical religious leader Ayatollah Khomeini had taken over as ruler of Iran, and it was under his leadership that revolutionaries seized the American hostages and imprisoned them in Tehran. Though a few were freed in the beginning, 52 remained in captivity for 444 days. Carter's plan to storm the embassy and free them failed when a plane and a helicopter collided in the rescue attempt, killing eight team members.

Fearful of further retaliation in Iran, Carter embarked on secret and delicate negotiations with Iran that would last for months. His main goal was to make sure the hostages would remain unharmed. Television newscasters would end their nightly news programs by flashing on the screen the number of days the hostages had been held. Counting the days became a national preoccupation, made more visible by the yellow ribbons pinned to trees around the country as reminders of the men in captivity.

Carter's popularity declined after his rescue mission in Iran failed and as unemployment and inflation in the

United States began to rise. Even his brother, Billy, began to embarrass him. Lampooned in the press as a bumpkin, Billy's drinking and rash public statements reflected badly on the president and damaged his image. But, as expressed in his memoirs, Carter stood by his brother with love and compassion.

Jimmy Carter is shown here with brother Billy in 1978.

Billy liked to take the other side of any argument, and could hold his own in defending an unpopular and sometimes bizarre position. . . . He also took advantage of the chance to present the other side of the Carter family—not so serious, full of fun and laughter. . . . Billy became a natural for talk shows and television comedy, . . . but he . . . began to depend too much on alcohol to keep him going. . . . He decided to face the problem squarely and try to overcome it, and became a patient at the alcoholism treatment center in Long Beach, California. He did extremely well. All of us who love him were pleased with his rapid progress and this proof of his personal courage.

Sensing the growing criticism of his own progress as president, Jimmy Carter appeared on television and addressed the "malaise" in America—the general discontent and "the crisis in confidence." Though the speech showed Carter to be truthful and forthright when speaking to the public (unlike his predecessor Richard Nixon), it did little to change people's feelings. Hoping to reverse the downslide, Carter fired many Cabinet members and hired fresh faces to replace them. But according to news analysts, such actions seemed desperate and could do nothing about the dark cloud that hung over the country—the hostage crisis in Iran. All of Carter's efforts during his last year in office were overshadowed by that event.

98

Throughout 1980, Carter and his staff worked at full speed to negotiate the freedom of the hostages and, at the same time, to campaign for reelection in November. Former California governor (and, still earlier, popular movie actor) Ronald Reagan was Carter's opponent. Riding on a wave of upbeat publicity, Reagan cheered up a somber America. In the campaign debates, he asked voters a key question: "Are you better off now than you were four years ago?" He made Americans think twice before reelecting Carter on November 4th. And when that day came, a majority of voters rejected Carter and elected Ronald Reagan as the 40th president of the United States.

"It seemed to me," Carter wrote in *Everything to Gain*, "that short of bringing the hostages home in a dramatic triumph just before voting day, there was no way we could have overcome the political damage caused by their extended kidnapping. The whole nation was obsessed with our failure to secure their release—and so was I."

Carter's disappointment in his defeat was profound. And to add insult to injury, the Iranians waited until Reagan took the oath of office before they released the hostages! Just 33 minutes after Reagan was inaugurated, the hostages were freed—and they came home safely and unharmed. Carter was thrilled,

After 444 days of captivity, the hostages arrive home in the United States in January 1981.

because it meant that his careful, behind-the-scenes negotiations had succeeded. But he had been robbed of the chance to welcome the hostages to the White House and to celebrate the homecoming he had so anxiously awaited and worked so hard to achieve.

Jimmy Carter

One question haunted the public and political analysts alike: Did Reagan engineer the delay of the hostages' return in order to prevent Carter's reelection? Many say the answer is obvious, but the question remains unanswered.

In his diary, Carter made a special notation about his last dinner party at the White House as president. That night, the Carters were once again honored by the presence of their friend, cellist Mstislav Rostropovich, who had played at the White House when the Camp David agreement was signed. While toasting Carter's achievements, he reminded the guests that sometimes the masses make mistakes. They made a mistake, he said, when they rejected Beethoven's Ninth Symphony, when they rejected La Traviata, and when they rejected Tosca. And, he concluded, they made a mistake in November when they rejected Jimmy Carter for a second term in office.

"He said history was going to treat [me] the same way [it] did Verdi, Puccini, and Beethoven," Carter wrote. "It was beautiful. . . . the kind of speech a defeated candidate likes to hear!"

In their book *Everything to Gain*, Rosalynn and Jimmy Carter looked back on their departure from the White House: "It had been quite a journey: to the state Senate and then to the governor's mansion . . . and finally to the White House. Now it was over—too soon, we thought. But it was over, and decisions had to be made about what we would do with the rest of our lives."

In retrospect, voters in the 1980 election may wonder if they paid too much attention to the looks of the candidates—the tall, presidential-looking Reagan versus the short and slender Carter. But as a keen observer noted: "Standing next to Reagan and Ford, Carter may look short; but next to Gandhi and Martin Luther King, Jr., there's no difference."

Chapter
12

Facing the Future

*D*espite his defeat, reporters noted, Carter appeared friendly and gracious when he left the White House. He looked forward to spending more time with Rosalynn—and having time to go fishing, too. But not for long. Though fishing had been a favorite pastime since childhood, it was not Carter's style to spend endless hours in a trout stream, except on weekends and vacations. But even then, he would have work to do as well. He was 56 years old when he left office, and as he recalled later, "I was not ready for retirement!"

Fourteen-year-old Amy was not happy to leave the White House. She hated leaving the good friends she had made in Washington. And who would want to leave a house that had its own bowling alley, movie theater, and indoor swimming pool? But Amy's parents assured her that there would be new—and old—friends and activities waiting for her in Plains.

Plains was more than a hometown to the Carters. It was the place where Jimmy Carter had always found renewed strength in times of stress. But this time, he soon discovered, would be different. On his return in 1981, he met a disaster almost as depressing as losing the election. His warehouse business, which had been so successful in the past, had been mismanaged in his absence and was a million dollars in debt! Without funds to revive it, Carter sold the warehouse, and with his earnings from books (he wrote five books in the first few years back in Plains), saved the family farm. With Rosalynn's help, he began to rebuild his life.

Carter enjoyed teaching Sunday School in Plains. In *Everything to Gain*, he recalled one session when the group discussed ways to find peace and joy in times of pain and defeat.

> *There was a general agreement that we should inventory our talents and interests, that our goals in life should be worthy as measured by God, that we should attempt things that might be beyond our abilities, and that this would put us in a spirit of submission to God's will. Once we do all this, we can then undertake worthy goals with boldness and*

confidence, realizing that these revised ambitions might be quite different from the more self-serving achievements we had previously coveted.

One of Rosalynn's first concerns on arriving in Plains was the condition of their home. No one had lived in the house for ten years, while they had been campaigning, living in the Governor's Mansion and occupying the White House. Some restoration and repairs were needed as well as new storage space for all their clothes, books, and other memorabilia accumulated in that time. But her husband's immediate concern was the building of a presidential library.

Since President Harry S. Truman left office in 1953, a presidential library—to house the historic documents, photographs, and other hallmarks of one's presidency—was expected to be built after a president left office. But Carter wanted his library to be more than a storehouse for documents. In *Talking Peace*, a special book for young readers, he wrote,

I was very concerned about building a library that would function not merely as a memorial to my administration but would be a workplace that would serve some greater purpose in the world.

Carter's goal—to ensure peace and human rights for all—was still on his mind, and as he had learned from the peace talks at Camp David, diligent research, discussion, and active involvement would be required to pursue it. There must be a way, he thought, to unite his vision of world peace with the purpose of a presidential library. As he wrote in *Talking Peace,*

> *Rosalynn remembers that I woke up in the middle of the night during this difficult time of transition and talked to her about building a center near the library where she and I could work on conflict resolution and some of the other issues that were important to us.*

In 1982, Carter's midnight dream came true, and the Carter Center was established at Emory University, where he is still University Distinguished Professor. Four years later the Center and the Jimmy Carter Library and Museum moved to a new location just a few miles away. Since its founding, the Carter Center has earned international praise for uniting people and resources in order to resolve conflicts and help erase hunger, disease, and violations of human rights around the world. Internship programs give college students a chance to research problems such as the causes of poverty and homelessness in America and elsewhere. The students learn from a staff of approximately 200 people, including experts, scholars, and world leaders who come to the Center in a spirit of

106

The Carter Presidential Center in Atlanta, Georgia

cooperation that has made the Center famous.

Carter believes that everyone has a right to decent food, shelter, and health care—the three "building blocks of peace." When these "foundations" collapse and the right to speak out is oppressed, people are bound to rise up and rebel. In a 1994 television interview with Charles Kuralt of CBS, Carter responded to critics who called his pursuit of human rights for all "naively idealistic."

Although it is idealistic, human rights are the cutting edge of societal change. When human rights are abused, it almost inevitably leads to a civil war. That's one reason we now have the greatest number of wars on earth of any time in history. . . . [When listing human rights] the average American will say freedom of speech, freedom of religion, freedom of assembly, freedom of the press, a trial by jury, that's it. [People in other] countries say that the right . . . to have a home, medical care, job, or food . . . might be human rights. But I think the proper thing is to define human rights in the broadest sense and not just selectively [to gratify] ourselves.

Carter likes to remind us that "the United States didn't invent human rights; human rights invented America."

The role of the peacemaker, Carter explains in *Talking Peace*, "is to settle differences through compromise and negotiation before they erupt into war." According to those he works with and the many leaders of foreign countries he has met with, no one is better suited to that role than Jimmy Carter. "Operating with a personable, casual intensity," Clayton Collins writes in *Profiles* magazine, Carter races around the world putting out political fires and calming down dictators. And even in his seventies, he shows no signs of stopping. "Like the Energizer battery," another reporter said, "he keeps on going and going and going . . . "

108

Chapter
13

World Peace Carter Style

*F*rom the Caribbean to the Red Sea, Jimmy Carter responds to calls for help in monitoring elections as well as in negotiating peace treaties. In recent years he has worked side by side with election officials and voters in numerous countries—including the Dominican Republic, Haiti, Panama, Nicaragua, and Paraguay—to make sure votes are counted correctly and no fraud or coercion takes place. But it is his role as mediator—or catalyst—in resolving conflicts that continues to attract attention and applause.

Writing in *Time* magazine, George Church calls Carter "the globe-trotting peace missionary . . . tackling the world's problems one by one." In North Korea, he won a promise from that government to stop bomb-related work in its nuclear power plants—

Jimmy Carter checks election ballots at a polling site in Port-au-Prince in December 1990 during the first free election in Haiti's history.

leading to a freeze on the nuclear program. In Haiti, he averted a U.S. invasion to oust a ruthless dictator by negotiating the leader's peaceful exit from the country; in Bosnia, he won a three-month cease-fire; and in Sudan, he won a two-month cease-fire in a 12-year civil war.

Students and professionals alike often ask, How does Carter succeed where others have failed?

Rosalynn and Jimmy Carter with North Korean officers at the conclusion of Carter's peace mission to North Korea

Typically, he credits the Carter Center for keeping him informed about troubled areas around the world. Armed with up-to-date facts, Carter is then prepared to go on a moment's notice wherever peace is in jeopardy or war is imminent.

But more profound clues to Carter's success can be found in his background—not only in his years in the White House, where important contacts were made, but also in the Deep South, where he grew up. With racial and cultural differences all around him, Carter always managed to find a bond between peoples. And at the root of all his success as a "missionary of peace," as Dr. Henry Kissinger calls him, is his deep Christian faith. "The missionary must be a missionary of love," Mother Teresa wrote, "must always be full of love in his soul and must also spread it to the souls of others, whether Christian or not." And Carter does.

But he has attracted some critics, too. "It is Carter's willingness to negotiate with the bloodiest tyrants, and even to praise and flatter them, that makes him the most effective—and most controversial," Church writes in *Time*. He even invited John Garang, the Sudanese rebel leader, to visit his Sunday School class in Plains! And he came!

Still others have criticized him for "helping to

legitimize a band of killers" in order to win the cease-fire in Bosnia, as Church reports. But, he concludes: "A former president with a zeal for foreign policy and a clear idea of what he wants can be useful to a current president. . . ."

Reporters often ask Carter: Is your free-lance diplomacy now motivated by your disappointing

Carter, working for a Bosnian truce, meets with President Milosevic in Belgrade.

113

foreign policy as President? In a May 1995 interview in *Profiles*, he seemed to put that question to rest.

> *I don't think there were any serious mistakes in our foreign policy. . . . We were obviously delayed . . . in getting our hostages back, but every single hostage came home safe and free. . . . As far as the Mideast, the Camp David accords are still the only basis for current negotiations. . . . We [normalized] diplomatic relations with China. . . . We kept our country at peace. We promoted human rights. I don't have any apologies to make about our foreign policy achievements. I don't have the slightest motivation to try to redeem something or to correct something.*

> *We obviously just try to do at the Carter Center some of the work that was unfinished when I was defeated for reelection. That's been the motivation for us.*

The Carter Center provides background material on world leaders for Carter to study prior to his foreign missions—as his White House staff once did before the Camp David talks and other negotiations. He learns about the leaders' political views, personal traits, and special problems, such as diseases and environmental conditions, currently affecting their people. Carter then stores the information in his amazing memory and, at the appropriate time and in his own quiet manner, dazzles the leaders with his thorough knowledge of the countries they rule. But it is his genuine concern for their problems—and his desire to solve them—that holds their attention. Sudan is a perfect example.

With Rosalynn at his side, Jimmy Carter went to Sudan in March 1995 to pursue a cease-fire in that warring North African country. The Task Force on Disease Eradication—a part of the Carter Center—had brought them up-to-date on the terrifying parasitic Guinea worm disease that had been killing 5 million people each year in India and Africa. (Guinea worms, whose eggs invade the water, grow inside a person's body after the person drinks contaminated water, and eventually crawl out through pores in the skin. If they die beneath the skin or are cut off as they emerge through it, fatal infections will follow.)

Backed by medical experts and armed with donated supplies of filters and chemicals to purify the water, Carter asked for a cease-fire in Sudan's civil war so that medical teams could move in and treat those suffering from the fatal Guinea worm disease while others could treat the water. Finally, after 12 years of fighting, both sides agreed to Carter's plan and laid down their weapons.

As the treatments began to take effect, Carter predicted that the Guinea worm disease would be completely gone by 1996. In typical Carter style, he credited others for his remarkable achievement. "Thanks to an extraordinary effort of international compassion and cooperation," he wrote in *Talking Peace*, "this story can have a happy ending."

Carter with Sudanese President Omar el-Bashir

Jimmy Carter

Not all of Carter's victories have taken place abroad. Both Rosalynn and Jimmy Carter feel as passionately about peace and human rights at home as they do about those issues for people in less fortunate countries. Their volunteer work on behalf of the poor and homeless, for example, is already legendary in America and continues to motivate thousands of other volunteers. Decent housing, Carter says, is a "building block" of peace.

Chapter
14

*H*abitat for Humanity

*A*nd my people shall dwell in a peaceable habitation, and in sure dwellings, and in quiet resting places.

—Isaiah 32:18

It seems shocking that in a rich country like the United States there are people living in the streets and under railroad bridges or waiting for beds in temporary shelters. "While it is true that some homeless people are lazy, and others are addicted to drugs [including] alcohol, many have only lost their jobs and are unable to afford a place to live," Carter wrote in *Talking Peace.* "Our wealthy society should realize that a decent place to live is a basic human right for all its citizens, especially for those who are unable to care for themselves."

But Jimmy Carter does much more than *write* about the problems of the homeless. He and his wife have made a commitment to do all they can to help the homeless help themselves. Wearing jeans and work shirts, the former President and First Lady wield hammers and other tools along with experts and volunteers

Jimmy and Rosalynn Carter work together on a Habitat for Humanity project in Atlanta, Georgia.

as they build houses from scratch for the poor and the homeless. Since the Carters joined Habitat for Humanity—a Christian housing organization that earns no profits and accepts no governmental assistance—thousands of other volunteers have joined, too. Staunch members since 1984, Jimmy and Rosalynn Carter work side by side with the future homeowners, who are a crucial part of Habitat teams. "By investing themselves in the building process," Habitat officials explain, "homeowners gain self-reliance, self-esteem, and new skills. . . . Through the houses we build, hope is restored and lives are changed as the cycle of need is broken."

Another great benefit of the Habitat projects is the community spirit they arouse. Working together for the good of the community results in less crime, less prejudice, less alienation, and more love, more joy, and more peace. "No matter how diverse our backgrounds, our hopes, our fears, our aspirations, or our concerns," Carter writes, "people find how much they have in common when their goal is to help others. I don't know of anything I've seen that more vividly demonstrates love in action than Habitat for Humanity."

In July 1994, Carter and 1,200 volunteers headed for the Cheyenne River Indian Reservation in South

Dakota to build homes for the needy there. "As I watched him hammering away on a house for an Indian family," a friend said, "I thought of that great Peter, Paul, and Mary song: 'If I had a hammer, I'd hammer in the morning, I'd hammer in the evening all over this land. I'd hammer out justice, I'd hammer out freedom, I'd hammer out love between my brothers and sisters all over this land.' Or something like that. Anyway, that's exactly what Carter was doing!"

But another Habitat experience stood out from all the rest that year: When the Flint River flooded the home of 77-year-old Annie Mae Rhodes in Albany, Georgia, she managed to save a picture of someone she had known and loved—Miss Lillian, Jimmy Carter's mother. Annie Mae was only 16 when she began working for Miss Lillian and Mr. Earl in 1933, and she cooked and cleaned for them for 22 years.

When Carter heard through the Red Cross that she had lost her home and belongings, he immediately went to work on a Habitat house for her and her ill brother. Surprised and overjoyed by Carter's arrival on the scene, Annie Mae said, "I didn't know what I was going to do. . . . I just prayed, and God opened doors." Despite arthritis in her legs, she pitched in and "painted, swept floors, washed windows, and helped hang wallboard," a local paper reported. The Carters built the frame and put up the roof trusses. To Annie Mae and the Carters, it seemed fitting that the boy she once took care of was now helping her rebuild her life. As a child, Carter was "quiet and well behaved," Annie Mae told a reporter. "And he still is."

Jimmy Carter has been honored many times for the progress he has made on the road to world peace. His awards include the Gold Medal of the International Institute of Human Rights; the International Mediation Medal of the American Arbitration Association; the Martin Luther King, Jr., Nonviolent Peace Prize; the Liberty Medal; and the Albert Schweitzer Prize for Humanitarianism.

When Carter is not engaged in holding meetings with world leaders or in building houses for the homeless, he is busy at home in Georgia, where he still teaches at Emory University, chairs the board of the Carter Center and its nonprofit affiliates, fly-fishes when he can, perfects his woodworking skills, listens to music—ranging from Beethoven to Bob Dylan—and visits with his family, which now includes grandchildren. Both Rosalynn and Jimmy Carter enjoy reading, and they continue to write. Rosalynn's new book, *Helping Yourself Help Others*, is a guide for caregivers and a source of strength for those who care for the elderly, the sick, or the disabled. She is honorary

Former President Jimmy Carter at a press conference in 1994

chairperson of the Rosalynn Carter Institue (RCI), a caregiving center in Americus, Georgia.

In 1995, Jimmy Carter surprised everyone when

his first book of poetry, *Always a Reckoning*, was published. His poems recall the segregated South, farm life, pastimes, politics, and love. Austin Straus reviewed the poems in the *Los Angeles Times* and captured the essence of the man who wrote them.

> *Few public figures even attempt poetry. Carter's work, despite its technical flaws, shows a warm, caring individual, a sensitive man I would love to meet and talk to. I came away amazed that such a kindly, trustworthy gentleman ever got to be president.*

Americans still watch in amazement as their former president, out of office for more than 14 years, continues to work toward his goals—turning words into actions, despair into hope, and war into peace.

Selected Bibliography

Carter, Jimmy. *Always a Reckoning*. New York: Times Books/Random House, 1995.

———. *Keeping Faith: Memoirs of a President*. New York: Bantam Books, 1982.

———. *Talking Peace*. New York: Dutton Children's Books, 1993.

———. *Turning Point*. New York: Times Books/Random House, 1992.

———. *Why Not the Best?* Nashville: Broadman Press, 1975.

Carter, Jimmy and Rosalynn. *Everything to Gain*. New York: Random House, 1987.

Carter, Rosalynn. *Helping Yourself Help Others*. New York: Times Books/Random House, 1994.

Germond, Jack. *Blue Smoke and Mirrors: How Reagan Won & Why Carter Lost the Election of 1980*. New York: Viking, 1981.

Lasky, Victor. *Jimmy Carter: The Man & the Myth*. New York: Marek, 1979.

Robinson, Earl, ed. *Young Folk Songbook*. New York: Simon & Schuster, 1963.

Robinson, Jerry, ed. *Best Political Cartoons of the Decade* (1970s). New York: McGraw Hill, 1981.

Periodicals

Church, George J. "A Peace Here, A Peace There." *Time*, April 10, 1995, pp. 46–47.

Collins, Clayton S. "Public Servant No. 1." *Profiles*, May 1995, pp. 23–26.

Habitat World 11 (Americus, Georgia) No. 3, June 1994, pp. 2–15.

Los Angeles Times, April 16, 1995, p. 10, Section BR.

New York Times, September 19, 1994 (National), pp. A1, A4.

Star Tribune, (Minneapolis), September 19, 1994, pp. 1A, 12A; September 20, 1994, p. 7A; November 29, 1994, p. 5A; December 24, p. 2A.

Television

"Biography: Jimmy Carter." Arts & Entertainment Network, April 11, 1995.

Carter, Jimmy. Interview with Charles Kuralt. CBS-TV, September 18, 1994.

Carter, Jimmy and Rosalynn. Interview with Forrest Sawyer. ABC-TV, January 12, 1995.

"Hometime." PBS, January 14, 1995.

*I*ndex

Always a Reckoning 26, 123

Begin, Menachem 89, 90, 91, 94
Bosnia 111, 113
Brezhnev, Leonid 80, 82, 83
Brinkley, Douglas 71
Brown, Harold 65, 83
Brzezinski, Zbigniew 66, 83, 89, 95

Carter, Amy Lynn 39, 60, 63, 81, 103
Carter, Billie 17, 34, 97, 98
Carter, Donnel Jeffrey (Jeff) 28, 32, 60
Carter, Gloria 17
Carter, James Earl, Sr. 16, 18, 21, 31, 32, 33
Carter, James Earl III (Chip) 28, 32, 42, 56, 60, 63
Carter, John William (Jack) 28, 32, 60
Carter, Lillian Gordy 16, 18, 20, 21, 26, 31, 34, 46, 47, 58, 63, 121
Carter, Rosalynn Smith 10, 17, 26, 27, 28, 33, 34, 38, 57, 58, 60, 63, 91, 101, 103, 104, 105, 106, 115, 116, 119, 120, 122
Carter, Ruth 17, 26, 38
Carter Center 10, 106, 107, 112, 114, 115, 122
Church, George 109, 112, 113
Clinton, Bill 10
Coleman, Julia 22, 46
Collins, Clayton 108

Deng Xiaoping 80, 81
Dole, Robert 55
Dylan, Bob 56

Egypt 9, 87, 91, 92
Everything to Gain 16, 17, 18, 99, 101, 104

Ford, Gerald 48, 54, 55, 57, 58
Fortson, Ben 43, 44, 49

Garang, John 112
Gates, Robert M. 71
Germond, Jack 49

Habitat for Humanity 9, 119, 120, 121
Haiti 111
Helping Yourself Help Others 122
hostage crisis 9, 95, 96, 98, 99, 100, 101

127

Hurst, Joe 36

inaugural address 58, 59, 60
Israel 9, 87, 89, 91, 92, 94

Jones, David 83
Jordan, Hamilton 50, 65, 89

Keeping Faith 47, 50, 63, 64, 66, 68, 74, 77, 84, 93
Khomeini, Ayatollah 96
King, Martin Luther, Jr. 14, 43, 44
Kissinger, Henry 8, 112
Kuralt, Charles 107

Lance, Bert 65, 77, 78, 79

Maddox, Lester 38, 44
Mondale, Walter 55, 64, 89
Moore, Homer 36
Nixon, Richard M. 48, 54, 58, 80
North Korea 109

Panama Canal 72, 73, 74, 75, 77
People's Republic of China 78, 80, 81
Perez, Carlos Andres 75
Playboy interview 56
Powell, Jody 65

race relations 10, 13, 14, 16, 18, 20, 30, 31, 34, 35, 38, 40, 41, 43, 45, 46

Reagan, Ronald 9, 85, 99, 101, 102
Rhodes, Annie Mae 121, 122
Rickover, Hyman 29, 30, 67
Rosalynn Carter Center 123
Rostropovich, Mstislav 92, 101

Sadat, Anwar 87, 89, 90, 91, 94
SALT treaties 78, 82, 83, 84, 85
Sanders, Carl 35, 40
Sawyer, Forrest 26
Seigneious, George 83
Smith, Allie Murray 26
Straus, Austin 124
Sudan 111, 112, 115

Talking Peace 105, 106, 108, 116, 118
Teresa, Mother 112
Torrijos, Omar 73, 74, 75
Truman, Harry S. 20, 30, 105
Turning Point 18, 20, 30, 35

Vance, Cyrus 65, 83, 89
Vietnam War 50, 66
Watergate 48, 50, 52, 55
Why Not the Best? 30, 36, 42, 43, 44, 49, 52
Woodcock, Leonard 80

Young, Andrew 66, 73